TOGETHER / APART
and other poems

TOGETHER/APART
and other poems

BY STEVE CLORFEINE

CODHILL PRESS

New Paltz / New York

ALSO BY STEVE CLORFEINE

Beginning Again

In the Valley of The Gods

Field Road Sky

While We Were Dancing

Codhill Press books are published by David Appelbaum
First Edition
Printed in the United States of America
© 2014 Steve Clorfeine.

ISBN 1-930337-82-5

Library of Congress Cataloging-in-Publication Data
Clorfeine, Steve.
[Poems. Selections]
Together/apart and other poems / Steve Clorfeine.
    pages ; cm
ISBN 1-930337-82-5 (alk. paper)
I. Title.

PS3603.L675A6 2014
811'.6--dc23

2014040604

To Jenny

Contents

Together / Apart

Postcards

Place

Together /Apart

HOW TO BE

Soen Nakagawa writes
All beings are flowers
Blooming
In a Blooming universe

away from the ledge
she steadies herself in his arms

they go on with their lives

down the block a man lies
propped against a wall
a dog wedged to his thigh
a small bucket between his legs
& a cardboard sign—
down on my luck

on upper Broadway facing north
hefty women in sleeveless dresses
lean their bulk
against a city bench
their various heads of
gray and dyed hair
wrapped in braids twists scarves
their necklines strung with beads

you will love yourself or stumble

complaints mount and the couple
rail against each other
the whole way round the children's zoo

together/apart
they hover like spiders

they drift
uncertain how far—
furlough or lifetime

return together
in penitence

the time of year when
box turtles
abandoned to migration
cross the road &

church bells
chime the quarter &
slowly raise the night

released from tangible evidence
this, that & because

he imagines his skin brushes hers
& hers brushes his in return

touch praises the way up
from bottom up &

it's possible again

the quiet
in a storm.

TIME

1.

he stares out the window
taps his fingers on the glass

this wakes the dog
who paddles over &
scratches the door
tail thumping on the wood porch

with the door now open
& the dog hustling in
a familiar breeze transports the man
seaside to a former romance

later
after an evening's reminiscence
he postpones his return
to anything
(*or anyone*)

afterwards
he writes of travels
fighting and dancing
from war zone
to holy place & back

even later
he says the watery distance
was always his natural longing
the amphibian delight
he'd always imagined:

going under, coming up
another way of surfacing.

2.

in conversations she
asks the perfect question
the one that gets him to say what hurts
(*the wisdom she reserves for children*)
she can do that for him

their exchange
though finely tuned
falls short
interrupted (*either one of them*)
withdrawn to unspoken thoughts
(*he knows only his own*)

in the end his commentary:
your blind eye
my deaf heart
(*to reflect on sorting out the blame*)

he remembers how
he brushes off kindness
like so much dust

he considers options
(remembered from ancestors):
seek a mikvah
submerge in ritual baths
imagine yourself purified
strained through a great sieve
another way to come clean

.

3.

alone again
he shelters
in his own arms
his own skin
remainder of a wilder nature

'*letting go is the logic of joy*'
he memorizes this phrase
repeats it / invites it

once more he slides across water
no reason not to seek happiness

happiness as kindness
& the other way round

in any case
a natural return:

another way of surfacing.

APART

1.

our world has marvels:
a mother's womb
a thatched roof
sweet chestnut trees
that line the drive
the storm that has an eye
the heart's magnetic field
its pulse
its mandala
its certainty that feeling
is a different sense than thinking

that ice fields move forward
as time does

2.

inside the cold flat he looks
& listens

cars buzz on the street

first snowdrops
first rhododendron buds
gray sky / yellow sky

thousands of miles
from your familiar curves

in the evening
church bells twice over
laundry folded
shadows in the back yard

where do we go from here?

3.

armed with dreams
with fading stars
frost meets my face
& dawn lifts

this frail moment
lifetimes apart

4.

you will be waiting to board at Heathrow
you will have bought a newspaper
you will not imagine how I long for you
in a TGV seat
cold chicken with wine
Paris bound
distracted by passengers who slip

up and down the aisles
flat green fields
& farm villages huddled together

5.

I draw a picture
with a story
it's you and somehow more

a larger whole
not yet visible.

TOGETHER

1.

where were you going that late
November afternoon
almost dark at five p.m.
surprised how fast the light goes

2.

one moves endlessly
towards & away

without bidding
things move
in subtle flexing

more or less
without bidding
we lean apart

not in distance
but in habit

3.

the great tree with the moon
visible through its branches
its branches made visible by moonlight
the capture or infiltration

that goes into making something
even a pie, I imagine
certainly a marriage

4.

when you turn the corner
my thoughts go back to a time
when I would have run after you
put my arms around you
chased you down like I once did
when you suddenly bolted
onto your bike / into a rainstorm
shopping bags of clothes in
one hand / steering with the other

5.

today we hang the laundry
stillness again
together

mice are dying in the walls
leaves begin to fall

our enterprise is shifting.

HOME

he prefers efficiency
despite which
in speaking
he takes a small point
on circuitous loops
each loop a distraction
from arrival or result

he admires the dry and wily way
a good English writer makes hay
of ordinary experience:

Simon Gray's *Smoking Diaries*
a memorable example
Bruce Chatwin, John Berger
Harold Pinter - the master

he takes satisfaction in detail
titles of books stacked
horizontal on a shelf:
Flora Britannica, Brilliant Moon
A Painter's Pilgrimage

brick chimneys beneath the clouds
peaked roofs with
small windows beneath the peaks

could it always be spring &
trees half done
with waxing leaves?

he thinks of groundhogs
living below the big rock
their life beneath the spreading shrub
his own underground passage

thunder peals
through open windows
as shopping lists
on scraps of paper
fly off the kitchen table &
stacks of sheet music
flutter on the piano top

content in her absence
among her things

does he see or dream like this
when she is present?

thunder again & children's voices

the local freight train
whose booming whistle
reminds his German friends
of the Wild West they'd seen
as children
in movie theaters.

NOTHING FALSE IN RETREAT
(After Wislawa Szymborska)

if not now then later

the wish
to continue
to go on with it
will return

now
under the covers
pillows propped
curtains drawn
phone off
heat up
door locked
now
finally

after false starts
after calling out
impersonator
fraud, fake

words sequestered
under blankets
& no one about
this falling daylight

what binds a person to events
when does mind leap beyond its boundaries
who returns happiness to its missing owner.

SEPARATE

wheat from chaff
white from black
the loves that lasted
longer than others
the wilting of desire

we go off & come back
roll &
cling together
curled in sleep

separation over time
over distances
in stages

like wallpaper or
linoleum tiles

one's humidity
has its effect on others

half the time
I'm steaming.

APRIL, THEN MAY

1.

The perfect color of daffodils
put your mind on that
he tells himself
noticing how easily he's pulled
to this or that crisis

the yellowy green of willows
buds / early bulbs
the way iris spike / reveal
their velvet folds

put your heart in that
he tells himself:
momentary and ever present
perfection.

2.

He goes back to see the peonies
early out this May
she hadn't asked
but as the bus draws near
he remembers her that summer
innocent / pregnant in a bikini

stared down by suburban wives
at the town pool.

3.

Fully formed / the peonies
prepare their brief perennial bloom
& we forget to worry

their collapse
in any downpour.

EARLY

morning mist on meadows
new bird feeder tucked onto the fence
above a stand of early blooms

first awake upstairs
a moment
just that

we are not so bad off in Spring
who pause in translucent green

whose children sip their lemonade
while even mothers wander off
to lean on trees

succulent & everlasting Spring

we stand in selfish skin
longing to be light
to be green translucent

suffused
not suffered

distilled
by sleight of season.

MAY

white gloves
pink azalea
dogwoods &
church on Sunday

it's Spring and
ice-cream trucks

it's Spring &
how to say it all before I forget

it's Spring & everywhere you turn
a feast appears to eyes &
phrases scatter

it's Spring & we recite the names:
jasper, poppies
wild viburnum
early blue violets
& wish forever

hallelujah spring

its twitters
its rise
display
arise

hallelujah spring
even the disasters of my thoughts
roll over dead.

BEGIN AGAIN, SPRING

1.

each day this Spring
he walks the north end of
Riverside or Central Park

a baseball field in North Meadow
where orange flags wave
on fences near home plate
the fine tan of baseball diamond dirt
prominent against the green
against the slate gray outcroppings

2.

trees beckon:

the plane tree with camouflage trunk
gnarled and naked limbs
shapes that draw the eye up
the leafy umbrella

the grand oaks whose limbs
line up symmetrical
span fifty feet
across the trunk

the catalpa which now in June
celebrates its
white orchidy flowers
petals dabbed in golden pollen
pathways brushed by vermillion dots

3.

how many times have you felt the sun
slip through clouds
and the first you know
it's like warm hands on your back
heat on your skin

a moment changes everything
whatever you were thinking
subsumed
in sensation

and would you miss that
if it never again happened?
and the algae in the pond
the cat-tails multiplied in broad clumps
the shrieks of children in the playground?

4.

like medical students
making morning rounds with doctors
six park rangers and apprentices
examine a lamp-post

under waving willows they
test the wiring that connects
the emergency phone box
its century old iron post
black against sullen rock

the six wear the colors of the park
green, gray, tan
pants, shirt, hat

they carry pads
pencils
buckets
and measuring tools

5.

a woman pauses with her dog
come on Baby
intimate
whispered to him alone
then more publicly, and to me

look they're following me

and there they are
dozens of sparrows peep and hop
on the ledge of the stone wall along the Drive
while the woman in a mock sad squeaky voice:
I have no bread for them

this is a big world
a woman, a dog, a flock of sparrows
traffic behind and in front and
looking up
those mighty oaks

later, down inside the park
on a bench and talking to Baby again
but stopping that conversation
to explain to me
about the latest flock of sparrows
(*or is it the same one from the ledge?*)
but interrupting that to tell Baby
who's chewing a piece of wood

no Baby, that's not for you
(the large tan curly ears droop over the just
dropped piece of wood, the eyes wide look)
and she, despairing
continues about the sparrows:

I shouldn't even come here if
I don't have bread with me
I shouldn't even come here

her high-pitched trill trailing off
as she turns away
while Baby waits on cue

this is a big world
a woman, a dog
a flock of sparrows
a witness

sheltering patches

moist and sweet loneliness.

WHAT'S LEFT BEHIND

1.

something to keep track of
like Betty's mother
records her solitaire victories
& defeats
in a spiral notebook

in the end
the notebook
the only thing
Betty keeps.

2.

he wills himself to accept the shrill cry - the
yapping of the Maltese mother & son next door
no worse he thinks
than noise inside his head
extemporaneous
barking mind.

3.

in the city he watches pigeons in
their gathering places
pigeons whose patterns & movements
recall urban uniforms:

firemen in rubbery black
chefs in herringbone slacks
kids in hoodies and watch caps
young women in spike heels and
plenty of flesh revealed

4.

later - away from the city
other birds come &
he assigns each species a character

a novice in naming birds
he'd begun late in life
had previously been more familiar

with choosing socks for example.

HERE'S WHAT HAPPENS

the dream - delicate & attentive
traced on light feet &
no predictable outcome
no damp jungle or culture to speak of

her moon is smiling

you lose the thread & the
fabric is still there

you remain in place &
what's a thread lost anyway?

crisp leaves on the sidewalk
sodden spinney wood behind the house

windfall apples mashed underfoot
the squirrel in the parking lot
flattened to a pelt

where once you came along
I lose you now each time I leave

the tide shifts &
the moon runs its course in the sky
night sings to moon
her glorious roundness
her slim & luminous arc

listen: I caress you
while the tide & sky are dancing
& the dream

how it doesn't sort out &
any odd moment pieces come back
& maybe the dream's
the true messenger

come back lovely specter
come face to face

come back lovely one &
tell me I'm on to something &

maybe the dream is
you're already home
& haven't noticed lately

the shape of you
without deflection &

don't tell me it's not true &
don't tell me it's not me

the moon
the dream

don't tell me it's not perfect.

Postcards

POSTCARD 1

Greetings from Cape Breton you write
re-claiming the broken down cottage
inland, off the Cabot Trail
North River near Baddeck

dampy days wanting no summary
is how you introduce yourself July 10, 1980

Cape Breton - discovered June 24, 1497
not Scots then but
spare and tough like Scots it was
nor by the way, did it have 184 miles
of paved highway
as the postcard says

A.J.'s down the road
is gone you say & we can't recall
was it a pub alone
or store and pub both?

more news is that
middle of the night
just when Alice phoned
thunder started up
continued with lightning flashes
until the connection cut out
and later the McDonalds' house
was struck

for me the maze of projects
frozen in place and some elements
of the event don't fade

along the Whycocomgh River
mossy green patches of land
that float like water
cold Atlantic rivers

the small rounded letters of your words

oysters of Whycocomgh

perfectly satisfying, you say.

POSTCARD 2

Mary Cassatt
(or the subject of her garden portrait)
flanked by tall blooming bushes
the foreground and background of the painting
set apart by the woman's white dress
her body fitted to a round wicker chair
arms raised, both hands holding a magazine

all this on a stamp
six swirling cancellation marks
that don't obscure the stamp's summer calm

I'd love to see or speak with you
an old friend writes on the card

a black & white photograph on the front
the profile of a thoughtful seated man
forearms resting on a sturdy wooden chair

could he live in the house next to the garden
where Mary or her subject sits
in the postage stamp image
on the reverse side

having caught a glimpse of the figure in a white dress
might he imagine her snug
in a wicker chair in the garden next to his?

in the photo he wears a white shirt, tie & vest
a ring on his left hand

shall we say he's handsome?
shall we imagine he's happily married
or perhaps not or not at all?

life has been a bit too full but with all lucky things
writes the friend

the man's room
sturdy and secure
potted plants on white cloths
calendar on the wall
a second wood chair &
a white door behind all this &

almost forgotten
an alcove with a window clouded over

I've thought of you many times over the years
wanting to be in touch.

POSTCARD 3

My dear L.
Kalua Road?

I've also changed address
but only temporary
Amsterdam, luchtpost
the old Queen's portrait
everywhere

On the postcard face -
Odilon Redon's painting of Pegasus
where mountain & sky meet
and there's the rider-less horse
floating in air

You describe a dream
that arrives in
unannounced fissures
wandering in a tropical forest of reflection

The horse rears it's hind legs and
digs into the mountain cloud
a blue cloud astride a somber mood of brown &
gray & the horse's eye so friendly

These dreams push us along
in the next one the white and black dog stands solicitous
as you re-paint a cabinet
stuffed with old shoes

Imagine us meeting in the Gemeente Museum
wearing clogs
speaking like Nederlanders.

POSTCARD 4

In a 1933 photograph by Paul Strand
she's called 'The Tailor's Apprentice.'

In Luzzara where she works
she wears a black coat buttoned to the neck
her mid-section covered by a large straw hat
held from inside so her hands don't show

(are they already tailor's hands?)

In Luzzara where she works
are they serious about the rise of the Duce?

She looks directly at the camera
her dark hair—Italian bob parted on the side
cropped below the ears
lines beginning to form on her young face
indents down the jaw
soft pouches below the eyes.

Beautiful Evelynne
who sends this card from Madrid
writes about wandering
falls asleep on a park bench
in the Botanical Gardens
then walks through the Reina Sofia Museum
and drinks beer in the cafeteria.

I like her even more for sending this portrait—
the dark-haired tailor's apprentice from Luzzara

And our long-distance dance continues
Evelynne & me.

POSTCARD 5

In my theater workshop
she speaks like one who's not lately
used the English language
in daily conversation

A mermaid in turquoise water
whose dancing torso shimmers

Hello and how are you?
the mermaid asks.

The print on the postcard:
In With The Fortune
Out With The Devil

Women in this woodblock
crawl in yardages of kimonos
looking for something on the floor or
delirious from mind-altering potions
formulas that reduce them earthbound in
silk designs of every pattern and color.

It would be nice to see you—
the mermaid again.

The 29 cent stamp has a white dove
inside a heart of roses
U.S.A. it says and L-O-V-E
in capital letters.

POSTCARD 6
(After a photo by Edouard Boubat)

she left him by degrees
at first, staying home while he visited friends
then closing the door to her room
the one she insisted was a study

when he got used to that
she began to sleep there most nights
and wake after he'd gone to work
or wander the streets before he woke
frequenting different cafes &
returning after he'd left

a few months before the departure
she grew silent &
though she still touched him
hoping to convey it was not his fault
the touch itself brought back what she hadn't expected
so she gradually refrained &
no longer met his gaze

in the end she left without packing very much
her life having already reduced itself

she wore the wide-brimmed straw sun hat
the one in the photograph from the island that last summer.

on one side there's Crazy Horse on a 13 cent stamp
on the other a guy called *Donkeyman* in a sombrero
a white shirt lettered GEORGIA across his chest

it's 1984, 16th April on the postmark
and Donkeyman
(*He-Haw* written after his name)
announces the 1980 Sugar Bowl champions
GEORGIA, the DAWGS, a perfect 12-0 record
and #1 over Notre Dame

There was a trip to Georgia
she writes from East Charleston Vermont and
I remember her in a poem I wrote in 1979
when I was falling in love & running around
doing a million things I don't do anymore

there are ponies in the high pasture and
I haven't told you yet that Donkeyman
leans on a donkey with baskets over its flanks
an American flag stuck in one of them

1984 I'm living on 21st Street
not falling in love anymore or
just starting it up again

my friend Collin will die that year, my father the next

the postmark stripes are fading from the
noble face of Crazy Horse
from the noble bygone loves
and the noble friend who writes
hope you're fine / love for now.

POSTCARD 8

Francesco touches the saint's fingertips
we know he's a saint
because of the halo
that crowns his gray pate

Francesco leans on a stick
his weight on his left leg
the right knee he bends
made prominent & sexy
by a one piece tunic that
reaches just below his crotch

I wish I could report all good news
the college professor writes from Firenze

the painting titled *The Tribute Money*
& Saint Peter will be advised
by Christ himself
how to get the dough

I have several heroic works-in-progress…
something different and quite grand

the walls of the Brancacci chapel, the
Basilica of Santa Maria del Carmine
mottled brown against Francesco's orange tunic
& the yellow robes of Saint Peter

nevertheless I'm running out of steam
and long for my own language

the painter—Masaccio
the first to paint shadows onto a fresco
was dead at twenty-six
one year after introducing
vanishing point perspective
to his work.

POSTCARD 9

She is present for us to see
& at the same time
by the light the painter has placed in her eyes
she sees something else.

The tip of her nose points to thin unsmiling lips
& though the portrait ends at her neck
we know that Martha Washington
painted by Gilbert Stuart
has seen a new world.

Around two sides of the 10 cent stamp the words
People's Right To Petition For Redress
a grim bust of Justice stands
hooded against a violet background.

Creamy skinned Martha floats on white canvas
her round face framed by a lacy colonial bonnet.

The card, printed in Germany
Bruder Hartmann, Berlin—commissioned
by Atheneum Museum of Fine Arts, Boston.

And Joseph, who sends love
long lost like the Thompson Street address
like the San Gennaro Festival
and the Italian-Americans he hung out with.

Flags are everywhere this Labor Day weekend
& we wave to each other in our American spirit:
Joseph, Martha, Gilbert, maybe even George.

POSTCARD 10

Mim W. writes to Mrs. Ola Forbes Wickham
from Dallas, Texas
having arrived there from San Antonio:

Nov. 11, 1949
unseasonable heat

it happens that my family is going west that month
in the brand new gray Nash
driving through Texas
on the way to Los Angeles
I'd be three in a week unaware of the weather

cool front coming in after heat and showers

unaware of the Cotton Bowl the next day
& whether Arkansas or S.M.U. is favored

Good thing I brought the overcoat

Mim W. ends the card in a p.s. after sending love
to Mrs. Ola Forbes Wickham

did the gray Nash stop at the Alamo in San Antonio?
did we see six flags
six nations that ruled the fort since 1718
one nation under God indivisible

this morning the Cooperstown High School students
listen to the pledge of allegiance
broadcast on the loud speaker

some pledge
some don't

on Mim W.'s postcard the one cent stamp is
marked with 5 lines of cancellation
the famous profile of George Washington & the reminder
Hire the handicapped: It's good business

one nation under God

this morning the President
declares his support for gay marriage
while the students mull over the writing
& half of them jump out of their seats & shout
when I ask how they feel about the President's statement

ran into wind, lightning and showers
from Denton to Dallas

Mim writes now from Norman, Oklahoma

where the waving wheat
can sure smell sweet
when the wind comes right behind the rain.

Place

S. KLEIN ON THE SQUARE

Rolled up under my arm I carry an Oriental carpet.
Intermittently I put it down - sit on it.
Contemplate nomadic issues:

Will the carpet serve me in all climes & terrains?
What if I have to haul it up a mountain?
If it gets wet & won't dry out?

My mother walks in front of me.
She's wearing a black dress with an eyelet pattern—
eyelets stitched in silver &
lime green satin lining.

Both high heels dangle from her right hand like
Sophia Loren in 'Two Women.'

I follow my mother
knowing she is complicit in this journey but
uncertain why we've set out or where to.

It's like going shopping with her as a child—
up the hill of shops on Broadway to the BMT subway line
above ground to Queensborough Plaza
then underground forever to Union Square.

Finally at the 14th Street stop
skirting Union Square park &
into S. Klein on the Square department store basement

past bins of women's underwear & brassieres (ugh)
my mother tugging me along to women's dresses.

Is the black dress with eyelets &
lime green satin lining
one she picked off the rack at S. Klein on the Square?

How unlike her to wear something so good
on a journey like this.

I remember then that the Oriental carpet
has a long story to it and I resolve to stay present
to follow the dream along.

We are and we are not who we are.
We are going back in time.
Back to shtetl forebears in the Pale of Belarus
going from place to place on dusty roads.

But why the high heels? Why the black dress?
In the end are we Italian?

Mother and son sit together on the carpet.
Its border of blue grapes and mother's
bare foot stretched out across a
delicately woven blue-green vine.

There is bread and oddly, peanut butter.
Might there also be
in mother's patent leather purse
a wedge of salami wrapped in waxed paper?

THE QUARRY

over smooth rocks
over watery crevices
on their bellies
the women slide

like creatures
who go silent
when approached

when alone
they splash wildly
propel themselves
off the rock face
into air
& fly or fall
downward
catch the waterfall
climb back up
triumphant &
fly down again

the women glide forward
rubbing bodies
their simple joy
sprung loose to
heap themselves
with pleasure

as their small herd
pivots in unison

their gestures becoming
to women / to creatures.

Dear Madam,

I am writing to tell you how much I admire the way you witnessed us - how your gaze held us so warmly.

I am one of those women.

Your kind laughter. Amused in the best sense of the word.

The pleasure you took in our movement which made us feel we could do nothing wrong.

Thank you from each of us women.

Please accept our deepest affection.

I'm certain that each felt something of what I attempt to describe.

And that small sigh of yours when we gathered with you at the end.

AH.

AROUND HERE

We love it when he's like that
forgetting his manners, his age.

Especially in the kitchen where it usually happens.
He's so familiar with the place—his acute sense of smell.

Olfactory Al we call him when he's not around—
when some scent or other reminds us.

Al squirbles.
Does a mean spin like a fish
defending itself with its tail.
You can almost smell sea water when he does it
and the splash—the flap of the tail muscle
right here in the room.

She - on the other side
pretzeled into that big old chair in the corner
her pokered thighs cushioned against the sidearm
bare feet dangling off.
Something illicit about those toes.

She's been the only woman in the house for years.
Who else would've stayed that long and
anyway both of them with bachelor brothers
and no love lost.

Now her, Lois—she would never squirble.
She's mostly quiet
remembers too much for her own good
she likes to say.

As usual all of us in the kitchen
the linoleum shiny & worn in patches.

Evening shadows which make the old
table and battered chairs less offensive.
Al & Lois less offensive.

We all blend in
end of another day.

Chirping & buzzing
through the screen porch.

Summer's like that around here.

DOWN IN THE VALLEY

1.

He plays pinochle on Wednesdays & Fridays
1 p.m. at the Valley Vista Adult Home & Senior Day
Care.

In bad games he's not sure he remembers
what the protocol is for dealing the cards.

In good games he's winning big
& his cousin Louie
whom he's secretly hated for decades
is taking a beating.

Good for you Louie
you bastard.

2.

Low hills surround hardscrabble and dust.
They're branding cattle in the pen & the long
deep lowing & sizzle of fried hair
penetrates their afternoons in the farmhouse.

He recalls their lives - the rough work
a square dance in town
a wedding - occasional release.
Sunday church.

Who would've guessed a guy like him
would fall in line -
& for love of what?

She's over sixty & there's no action between them.
Hasn't been for years.

He's not one to stir things up
so he keeps it to himself.
His needs - the fantasies that rotate
like winter and spring crops.

He stays.
Unannounced to himself or to her.

They laugh sometimes.
Look out the window at the dogs -
what they're doing now.

There's the weekly newspaper
a phone call from her brother
or his niece in the city.

That picks things up for a few hours
& they recall bits of it weeks -
even months later.

Especially in winter when work is slow
& dark early.

PLACE

cornerstone in the corner
where it should be

inset on granite
the large block dated June 13, 1914
inscription barely legible

once there was a long gravel road
bungalows on either side
pastel shutters against graying pine boards

this evening
swirls of insects surround a
single street lamp near the bench where
an old man sits &
holds a manual on table-saw safety
stares at the pages on his lap

past the bungalows a half mile down
the road becomes dust
empty save a small pond
brown with mud

above the pond
stars swim under heavens

a family of newts puddle about
from time to time
leap through the mud
plucking and chewing
bits of algae & grass

their acute night vision
& the pair of us watching
surprised by the sound of them by
what sensations the newts might be having
inside their shining skins

the same pair of us
circumambulates the pond
certain and clockwise

it takes a few slow minutes

the whole of this unexpected
unplanned

we are content
we are trousered and
full of dark wind &
departure
still ready for the next pond

or any further enchantment.

NOTE

Thanks so much for letting us stay here while you were
gone. Everything went smoothly.
Perfect really.
There was a small matter of birds banging themselves
against the windows.
We inquired at the local bird store & were told that the
male species sees its reflection in the glass and
determines to protect its territory.

I remember you saying something about bluebirds
doing that one year & how you would run outside
every time you heard a thud & wait patiently until the
bird revived & if it didn't you'd hold drops of water to
its beak.

Well this year it was goldfinches & I did just what you
described with some success.

You mentioned not to befriend the deer & we didn't.
But a family of rabbits began to nest under the old shed.
The offspring were pretty cute darting about
though we felt guilty enjoying them since we were
so pleased about your Jerusalem artichokes before
the rabbits & said offspring ate most of them & they or
groundhogs ate the coreopsis & also your euonymus
transplants which we'd been watering daily.

So sorry for all that.
You must be quite used to it.

Your phone messages are next to the answering machine.
Mail is more or less sorted. Took your advice & threw out
all the circulars & fourth class stuff.

We subscribed to the Little League in your name when
a very cute kid came around with envelopes.
You're now a sponsor of Mindy's Art Supply team.
They're calling themselves 'The Artful Dodgers.'

Thought you'd like that being a Brooklyn boy.

Oh, & an urgent sounding message from the National
Endowment for the Arts.
The grant category you applied for doesn't exist
anymore. Would you phone or fax them.
Ask for Rosemarie Headly, Todd Lesser, Kevin Bismatta
or Miriam Kantankrowitz.
They left all these names because some are moving on—
probably even as I'm writing this.
And please consider applying again they suggest.
In only three years your category might return to the
roster.

Acknowledgements

Designed by Liza Matthews

Editorial consultant: Katie Yates

Cover Photo: "Barcelona at Noon" and author photo
by Christine Alicino (www.christinealicino.com)

Steve Clorfeine is a writer, performer, director and coach with a long association to The Naropa University in Boulder, Colorado, and the State University of New York. As an independent workshop leader, he presents training programs for teachers, performers, business leaders and at meditation centers throughout North America, Europe and Asia.

Steve has ongoing collaborative relationships with colleagues from the disciplines of theater, dance, music and visual arts. He is a founding arts faculty of the Authentic Leadershop Institute and of Naropa University.

In 2008 and 2009, he was awarded Cultural Envoy grants from the U.S. government to create theater pieces in Calcutta, India and in Kathmandu, Nepal. In 2014 he was awarded a Fellowship from Vermont Studio Center for his installation/performance "Correspondence," which opens in 2015 at the Westbeth Gallery in New York City.

Steve teaches twice a year in Europe and regularly in New York. He has been a student of Buddhist teachings since 1974. Steve lives with his wife in Kingston, NY and in New York City.